INNER REFLECTIONS

Kimmora Ward

Copyright © 2020 Kimmora Ward

All rights reserved.

ISBN: 9798673657898

DEDICATION

I dedicate this book to my Creator and close family and friends.

They form my support system.

"You will not arrive at Destiny's door if you do not take the first step."

CONTENTS

Dedication	iii
Acknowledgments	8
A Place of Love	9
Love	10
My Heart	11
Active Love	12
Active Love II	13
Love Thoughts	14
You and Me	15
Mesmerized	16
I Miss You	17
Life	19
Emancipate Me	20
Is it Possible	21
Speak Your Truth	22
It comes Naturally	23
Resonate	24
Livelihood	25
Freedom	26
God Cares	27
Star Sign	28
My Mother	29
Classy	30
Extraordinary	31
Names	32
Spirituality	33
Protection	34
The Seaside	35
I Can't Breathe	36
Black Lives Matter	37
2020	38
Me	39

Never Forget	40
Go Away Corona	42
Covid-19	43
Covid Days	44
About the Author	45

ACKNOWLEDGMENTS

I would like to acknowledge my mother Paulette Ward, the woman who has nurtured me since I entered this Universe.

Lorraine Hoyte who inspired me to create this collection and Alicia Abdullah who was my accountability partner throughout the whole process.

I would also like to acknowledge Yasmine White who gave her input on my poems. Special acknowledgement to all who support me in whatever I do, you know who you are.

A PLACE OF LOVE

I come from a place of love
You come from a place of love
We all come from a place of love
It is a place where there is no strife

No war
No disharmony
We are here on earth to learn
And transition back to this place
Do your part in this realm
Carry out service

Do goodwill
Build friendships
We are going back to the place
We are preparing for the place
We are beings of love
So let us do ourselves a favour and love!

LOVE

Love, would make a sweet name
If I bare a daughter that is what I'll name her
Love is special although sometimes irrational.
Do you love?
How do you show your love?

Is your love shallow? Or is it deep?
Do you sow or do you reap?
One last question, did you know that God is love?
He loves you and me.
This is a decree!

MY HEART

You can have my heart
Being mindful not to tear it apart
I am not the one to be played
This will make me dismayed
If I give you my heart
We can make a start

A family maybe
Will occur on our journey
Let's give each other our heart
So we will never be apart
This world is cold
But we will love until we are old.

ACTIVE LOVE

Prepare your love
So you can share your love
Believe in love
So you can receive ones love

Show your love to the ones you love
Even those who refuse to accept it
They will regret it, you will receive a feeling in your spirit
That is fit

When you are down to the ground
You will remember who showed you love soo profound
They may not be around
But when they were you were as happy as a clown

ACTIVE LOVE II

Making love is an action
Done to create satisfaction
Matchmaking nowadays is not an in thing
People choose to just have a fling

One must be careful of the Dis-Eases
They can leave boils within your creases
Even doctors cannot discover
Remedies to make you recover

Basically, I am saying to stay protected
Get connected
Make love the right way
In so doing you and your lover will stay!

LOVE THOUGHTS

What is love to you?
Do you think it should be pursued?
Or subdued, so you can review
Before you get entangled?
Love is tricky

It can be quite dodgy
You have to be skilled and strong willed
The uphill climb may be worth the while
But all in all if love is not
For you don't answer its call

YOU AND ME

People have their own complexities
Everyone has their own reality
You are responsible for yours
I am responsible for mine
I can wine or dine

I can have a say or two
Take extra care of myself when I have the flu
I don't prefer to be blue
I vibrate on a frequency so high
So high that it touches the sky

MESMERIZED

When I look into your eyes
I see a world filled with surprise
I behold the flawless depth of your soul
As it unwinds down the staircase of your heart
I am comforted by the stare of your warm eyes
As they caress my skin with care and attention

We walk hand in hand along the coastline
Beholding the rich sea green colour of the vast ocean
In the distance
We vow to each other that the feelings in our heart
Will last until we depart this earth
If one is to go before the other we would have
cherished the moments we spent together

I MISS YOU

What I do when I miss you
I think and think, I envision
I visualize until I finally realize that I have No need
to be blue
You are in a different time space but we will reunite
Once again

It must happen
What I desire is for us to be together
Enjoying the company of each other
This will come to pass
This will come true
God, I'm depending on you to make this desire
Come through!

LIFE

Life is short
Look within
Stay positive
Stay grounded
Don't become complacent
Serve, serve as if you would receive an award
Your reward would be to live eternally because
Life is short but your soul will exist forever!

EMANCIPATE ME

What do you know about me?
You cast judgement by what you see!
You must be shocked when I rise above expectation!
It surprises you and the nation.
Don't expect me to be remorseful
Rather, I'll be forceful
To call out any wrong
Done to me in this community;
These statements are not meant to exalt me
But rather to emancipate me
From the mental slavery,
What mental slavery?
The one established from lack of bravery!

IS IT POSSIBLE?

Is it possible to climb the ladder?
To get my heart's desire?
To acquire, acquire all of life's coming attractions?
Yes it's possible

It's possible to achieve
Achieve and receive blessings
Blessings from up above which only come down
Because of God's love

So act as if it is possible
Position yourself to be receptive
Of all that God has in store for you
He will never make you blue!

SPEAK YOUR TRUTH

We must all speak our truth
No matter what, speak your truth
Who are you hurting, bottling up your feelings
Inside?

You are doing a disservice to the spirit which abides
Abides within you
Too often do we let our Ego shout and exclaim for
Us to remain quiet

Or it would say, let them have their way
It is time to take a stance, take a chance and speak
Your truth!

IT COMES NATURALLY

It comes naturally!
Have you ever wondered why something comes
Naturally to you?
Have you ever thought that is what you were meant
To do?

Most humans do not walk there authentic path,
Rather they prefer to stay in a job
That often leads them to wrath
Do not be one of those people

Do your craft, If it is to draught, draught but
Do not become one of them who does not do what
Comes naturally because
Really you will be hurting you, not me!

RESONATE

It resonated with me so I spoke about it.
It resonated with me so I thought about it.
I deciphered the information and took what I could
Use
What I couldn't I simply put in refuse.
Some happenings are seen as coincidental but trust
Me,
Every happening is fundamental
Be open minded and explore the complexities of this
World.
When you seek it the truth will unfold.

LIVELIHOOD

When I was a child
I wasn't considered to be wild
I was the type who shined
I didn't make my parents whine

They were proud of me
I made their hearts smile with glee
I found comfort in doing this
It brought me nothing but bliss

Now I am an adult
They get the same result
Nothing has changed
Just my age

FREEDOM

Do what you want!
Take the path that you wouldn't regret
So that you wouldn't fret when you find yourself in a Bind

One that you cannot unwind from
It would be so frustrating and considered to be a sin Thing
So do what you want!

Come when you want, go when you want,
Buy what you want, sell what you want
The only advice I would give is for you to try and Live

Live within the rules of the land, if you don't,
You wouldn't be saved, not even if you were a Magician with a wand!

GOD CARES

It is in the atmosphere
As the wind kisses my skin
I feel his care
Yes my God is real

He will never neglect me
On the contrary, He will quickly free me
He will not allow me to go over a precipice
He will protect me from all the injustice

I will sing unto my God
Come into my heart
Without you I cannot start
Start any day, in any way

STAR SIGN

What's your Zodiac Sign?
I'm a Cancer
No, I do not have Cancer
That's the name the sign is under

I'm ruled by the moon
Sometimes this causes me to act the fool
As any other sign in the zodiac
I have my ways in which I act

Although I am a Cancer
My moon sign is Aquarius
When I found this out I was like
With this mixture, I can be very courageous!

MY MOTHER

I have a mother like no other
She's been mine for a lifetime
I share her but that's not a bother
She was nice enough to give me a brother

We have our disagreements
But they quickly dissipate
That's how well we relate
She's more than just a mother, she's my mate

I couldn't ask for more
She is even humorous, never a bore
She cooks, cleans, sews
How much I love my mother, only God knows!

CLASSY

Sometimes I'm classy
Sometimes I'm flashy
Sometimes I'm elegant
And at all times I'm relevant

I'm fond of self- care and I love me without fear
When I walk the streets a guy may stare
But I just give them the glare

Health is of paramount importance
I do not use any substance
I rely on the Almighty
What a Creator, He created me!

EXTRAORDINARY

Be willing to be weird
Be willing to stand out
Be an extraordinaire
Be someone who people talk about
Not all of us are the same

All are called by a different name
Wouldn't it be just a shame
When we give others the blame
When we blame them for us not achieving, believing
And receiving our greatest burning desires

What is required is that we persist until out desires
Cannot resist,
Resist to fall right in our laps
We would be happy gyals and chaps

NAMES

There's so much in a name
Character is in a name
Morales are in a name
Values are in a name
Love is in a name
Care is in a name
Quality is in a name
Charisma is in a name
Meaning is in a name
What is your name?

SPIRITUALITY

Be more spiritual than religious
Anyone can follow a set of laws and conform
But it takes more depth to look within and create a
Peaceful life

To which one can live with forever
Being spiritual means blocking out the constant
Noise that the world makes
And listening to your inner being

Making decisions based on your intuition and
Keeping the promise to yourself that
No matter what you are going to be there for you.

PROTECTION

Protect me from my enemies
Protect me even from myself
For destruction does not always come from
Someone else

Destruction can come from the enemy within
Guard my mind against the negative weeds and
Allow me to plant seeds of
Greatness and good morale

I will harvest a blessed return on investment when I
See to it that my time is well spent
Studying your word, building my character and
Serving so that I will be served in return

THE SEASIDE

Sometimes I wish my house was right by the seaside.
There would be a wonderful place to reside
I wouldn't mind the waves crashing when the ocean
Gets rough
Just hearing that would be more than enough
To make my sleep so deep and sweet
God really did an excellent job creating the earth, the
Cosmos and all reality but what I'm most thankful
For it is the crystal clear water, which when the sun
Hits it, it glistens, the sand that surrounds it, the
Creatures that inhabit
Yes I'm thankful for the seaside.

I CAN'T BREATHE

I don't think the hurtful soul on your neck
Understood your cry, "I can't breathe"
Was it that he wanted to prove a point?, but prove a point to who?

The others with him?
The same souls who did nothing to help you
In your utter turmoil and pain as you gasped "I can't breathe"

I believe your mother was crying for your
Deliverance where she was, it was as if her crying
Caused
You to call out for her, "Mama", but all of this could
Not save you from your deadly fate

He would try to prove a point by remaining on your
Neck shouting at you to get into the car but you will
Never get to move again as your lifeless body would
Remain, You could not breathe!

BLACK LIVES MATTER

I have a dream that someday American Society will
Realize that black lives matter,
So that if I decide to go for a jog around the
Neighbourhood I would not be shot in broad
Day light because I was black and looked like
Someone who committed a crime!
It would also be great if I can sleep in peace and not
Be shot eight times and don't talk about the privilege
Of being able to breathe.
I have a dream that someday everyone in America
Will realize that not only does all lives matter but
Black lives matter!

2020

Twenty-Twenty was supposed to be your year right?
But it arrived with Corona which caused soo much
Fright!
Then there was the unrest in America as a result of
The brutal death of three beautiful souls
As I write this poem I wonder what next?
Twenty-twenty was supposed to be fancy, not with
All this nonsense as if someone was working
Necromancy!
It's as if 2020 decided it's going to be ten years in
One, with all that's going on.
To the hills it wants us to run
Trials and tribulations have just begun
It is only June and 2020 has the hearts of men
Ruined.
Yes, you have broken our hearts 2020, guess we'll
Have to make a new start 2021.

ME

I am a young black woman with an elegant aura and
High vibrations
I feed off of positive vibrations and healthy
Circumstances
My inspiration comes from inside, yes; I was born
With the feeling to rise,
An element of surprise is always in my eyes
I thrive and possess fire inside that cannot be cast
Down by remarks oh so snide.
I will fix and wear my crown, so proud, even in my
Darkest days I will not let you see me frown.
I am a young black woman, proud of where I come
From!

NEVER FORGET

Have we forgotten Breonna?
Have we forgotten Aumaud?
Have we forgotten George?
It seems we have

We don't hear the talk anymore
It's always how the story unfolds
We as people sensationalize an occurrence and as
Soon as some time passes
It is but in the distance

Let us remember all our brothers and sisters who
Were treated unjustly, let us empathize
And sympathize with their loved ones and treat
Them with dignity.
Let us never forget all those who are gone for
Eternity.

GO AWAY CORONA

We didn't expect you
Why did you come?
I suppose you thought we were having too much Fun!
I suppose you thought we like to run!
Run to our houses where we'd have to stay a while
Many say, "Corona mussi tink me a chile!"
Didn't you know we would fear?
Didn't you know this is a huge scare?
But you came anyway
Today, I'm simply asking you to GO AWAY!!

COVID-19

COVID ALERT!
COVID ALERT!
Live life for what it's worth
People are dying
Families are crying
This virus is contagious
On a scale of one to ten it's 10
Very dangerous!
Stay inside where you reside
Yes it may be hard
But would you rather be marred?
Would you rather risk your life or be one of the
Many who will survive.
Walking this earth should not be taken for granted
We must unite, do what is right,
Fight COVID because this is warranted

COVID DAYS

Every day feels like Saturday
Everyday I'm sad because I want to go out and play
But I cannot because Corona would not go away
When are you going to leave?
Can you imagine the grief that we feel?
We are trying our best but you are putting us to the Test
Corona it's my advice that you take a rest
We want to live without the fear of you
But like a bulldozer you come barging through
Disrupting us and our livelihood
Please exit! I wish you would!

ABOUT THE AUTHOR

Kimmora Ward is an Auditor by profession and is employed by the Government of Montserrat. She is an avid reader and is mostly interested in content relating to Personal Development and the Arts. This is her first piece of work.

Printed in Great Britain
by Amazon